W9-CCW-674

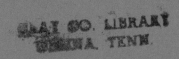

On the Mall in Washington, D.C.

On the Mall in Washington, D.C.
A Visit to America's Front Yard

Brent Ashabranner • Photographs by Jennifer Ashabranner

Twenty-First Century Books   Brookfield, Connecticut

Published by Twenty-First Century Books
A Division of The Millbrook Press
2 Old New Milford Road
Brookfield, Connecticut 06804
www.millbrookpress.com

Library of Congress Cataloging-in-Publication Data
Ashabranner, Brent K., 1921–
On the Mall in Washington, D.C: a visit to America's front yard/Brent Ashabranner; photographs by Jennifer Ashabranner
p.   cm.
Includes bibliographical references and index.
Summary: A guide to the monuments, memorials, museums, and gardens on the National Mall in Washington, D.C.
ISBN 0–7613–2351–1 (lib. bdg.)
1. Mall, The (Washington, D.C.)—Juvenile literature.   2. Washington (D.C.)—Buildings, structures, etc.—Juvenile literature.   3. Mall, The (Washington, D.C.)—Guidebooks—Juvenile literature.   [1. Mall, The (Washington, D.C.) 2. National parks and reserves. 3. National monuments. 4. Museums.] I. Ashabranner, Jennifer, ill. II. Title.
F203.5.M2 A84 2002
917.5304'42—dc21   2001041463
5 4 3 2 1

Contents

The Mall is the nation's ultimate civic space—a beautiful telling of the national story with grass, trees, water, bronze, and stone.
—Benjamin Forgey,
The Washington Post

The Mall—that splendid corridor of grass and trees that opens up the heart of this great American capital.
—Edwards Park,
The Smithsonian Experience

1 A Special Place

Through the years the National Mall in the heart of Washington, D.C., has been the subject of many beautiful thoughts and words. The Mall has been called "the Great Park of the American people" and a "pageant to over two hundred years of American history." It has also been called simply "America's front yard."

Hundreds of school groups visit the Mall every year and at all times of the year. Here a sixth-grade class from Gordo, Alabama, on a February visit in 2001 finds the Grant Memorial a good place to pose for a picture.

The original Smithsonian Institution Building, completed on the Mall in 1855, is popularly known as the Castle. It serves as an information center for the Institution.

I don't know how many times my daughter Jennifer and I have been on the Mall, but my guess would be well over a hundred. Several of our books have been about the great memorials on the Mall. For several years Jennifer worked as a volunteer for the Smithsonian Folklife Festival that is held on the Mall every summer. When I was with the Peace Corps in Washington, I sometimes walked to a lovely part of the Mall called Constitution Gardens to eat my brown-bag lunch under the elm trees.

But when Jennifer and I decided that we wanted to write and photograph a book about the Mall, we began by taking another walk. We started one April morning at the Ulysses S. Grant Memorial where the Mall begins in the east at First Street, and we walked to the Lincoln Memorial where the Mall ends in the west, almost on the bank of the Potomac River. Jennifer didn't carry a camera, and I didn't carry a notebook. On this day we just wanted to take in the Mall—to walk, to look, and to get the feel of the Mall back into our bones.

The Mall is bounded by Constitution Avenue on the north and Independence Avenue on the south. You can begin at any spot on the Mall and walk in any direction and almost immediately you are in a very special place. We walked through the delightful National Gallery of Art Sculpture Garden. Tourists there were pointing their cameras at Alexander Calder's metal sculpture, *Cheval Rouge*. We came to

Alexander Calder's metal sculpture, Cheval Rouge (Red Horse).

MORE ABOUT . . .
The District of Columbia

The D.C. in Washington, D.C., stands for District of Columbia. The District of Columbia is neither a state nor a part of a state. It is a unique federal district, 10 square miles (26 square kilometers) in area, created to contain the capital city of the United States. Many government agencies and offices are located in the capital district. So are embassies of governments from all over the world.

The National Mall is at the heart of this federal district. Behind the Grant Memorial and overlooking the entire Mall is the U. S. Capitol, the home of the U.S. Congress. Behind the Capitol is the U.S. Supreme Court. Joining the Mall at the Washington Monument is a grassy park. Toward the end of this park is the White House, home of the president of the United States. The design of the City of Washington and the National Mall was largely the work of architect Pierre Charles L'Enfant (lon-FAUNT).

the dramatic red Castle of the Smithsonian Institution, the first building constructed on the Mall, almost a century and a half ago. A large school group was going into the building, undoubtedly to find out about goings on at the Mall. Today the Castle serves as the information center for the sixteen museums and galleries of the Smithsonian Institution, nine of which are located on the Mall.

Jennifer and I walked slowly through the gardens surrounding the Smithsonian Castle and on toward the Washington Monument. I have sometimes had the feeling when I am on the Mall that this gleaming white marble obelisk contains a magic magnet that draws me to it. The monument rests on the top of a hill. To stand on this hill and look north to the White House, west to the Lincoln Memorial, south to the Jefferson Memorial, and then east to the Capitol is one of the great Mall thrills.

Just south of the Washington Monument is the Sylvan Theatre, an open-air stage in a grove of trees. The Sylvan presents plays, concerts, and other programs during the summer. Beyond the Washing-

The Washington Monument seen from the Mall Reflecting Pool. The slight change of color on the monument above the 152-foot (46-meter) level resulted from the use of marble from a different stratum.

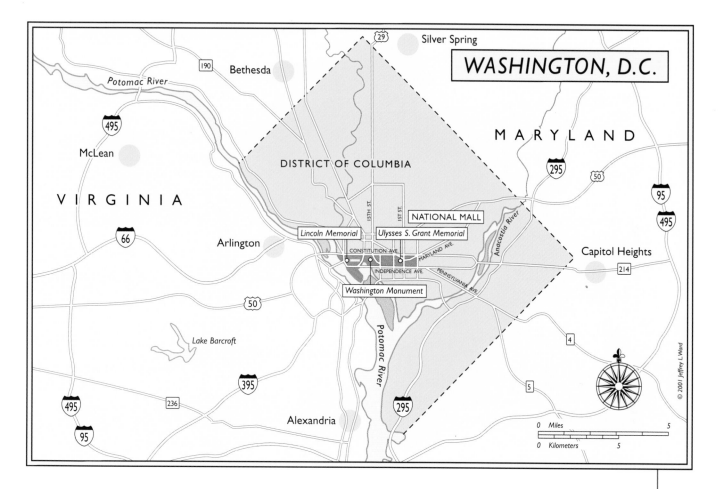

ton Monument, a reflecting pool 2,000 feet (610 meters) long and 160 feet (49 meters) wide stretches toward the Lincoln Memorial. On each side of the Reflecting Pool is a wide pebbled path shaded by large elm trees. Comfortable benches along the paths invite visitors to rest. Many people were on both paths this day; some sat on the benches watching gulls from the nearby Tidal Basin float peace-

In 1777 Pierre Charles L'Enfant left his native France and came to America to join the colonists in their War of Independence. Later, L'Enfant settled in New York. When he learned that a capital city for the new nation was going to be built on the bank of the Potomac River, L'Enfant wrote to President George Washington asking if he could help in creating a capital "magnificent enough to grace a great nation."

Impressed by L'Enfant's ideas and enthusiasm, Washington asked the eager architect to begin work on plans for the new city. As a first step, the president invited L'Enfant to join him in a visit to the newly created District of Columbia, then just a large tract of rural countryside where the capital would be built.

During the month of June 1791, Washington and L'Enfant walked the land, admiring the beauty of the gentle hills and valleys, discussing the possibilities, taking notes. On one of those days they stood upon a rise known as Jenkins Hill. L'Enfant was overwhelmed by the view, especially looking westward toward the Potomac. Here, he declared, the Capitol of the new nation should be built. He later called Jenkins Hill (known today as Capitol Hill) "a pedestal waiting for a superstructure."

The enthusiastic L'Enfant set right to work designing the city of Washington, not even waiting for a contract from the government. The city would have wide avenues radiating from the Capitol and from the president's house, with many parks, squares, and circles placed throughout the business and residential areas. A grand avenue (now known as Pennsylvania Avenue) would connect the Capitol with the president's mansion, which would be located about a mile to the northwest. In his vision, L'Enfant saw a "vast esplanade," a great grassy mall, 400 feet (122 meters) wide running for about a mile directly westward from the Capitol and ending with a monument to George Washington.

L'Enfant completed his plans of the proposed federal city within six months, but in February 1792 he was dismissed as design architect. He had refused to make compromises and was unable to get along with the city commissioners who were responsible for the project.

For most of the nineteenth century L'Enfant's plans for the city of Washington and the National Mall were largely forgotten. Private citizens grew vegetables and grazed cattle on the Mall. Public markets were held there. The Baltimore and Potomac Railroad was permitted to lay tracks on the Mall near the Capitol.

Then a dramatic return to L'Enfant's vision for Washington began in 1901. In that year a Senate commission headed by Senator James McMillan of Michigan was given the responsibility of redesigning the nation's capital. Senator McMillan named some of America's most outstanding architects and landscape specialists to the commission. Their work was strongly influenced by L'Enfant's original plan. One of the McMillan Commission's decisions was to extend the Mall westward to the Potomac River. It was there, at the western end, that the magnificent Lincoln Memorial would later be built.

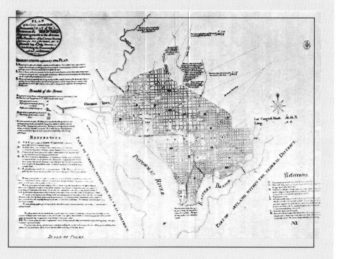

During his lifetime L'Enfant was neither recognized nor rewarded for his work. But today the great Capitol and Mall of which he dreamed are the spiritual heart of Washington—the capital city of the great nation that L'Enfant loved.

L'Enfant's plan for the capital city

At the Lincoln Memorial on Lincoln's birthday, young visitors look thoughtfully at the statue of the Great Emancipator.

fully on the quiet water of the Reflecting Pool.

We walked on the north side of the Reflecting Pool. Occasionally through the trees on the other side, we could catch a glimpse of one of the stainless steel statues of the Korean War Veterans Memorial.

By the time we reached the Lincoln Memorial, the Mall was very much back in our bones. We sat high on the memorial's steps and looked back over our walk. It is not such a long walk, a bit less than 2 miles (3 kilometers), but every step is unforgettable. No wonder the Mall draws approximately 21 million visitors each year. As we sat there, I reflected on the different ways people have described the Mall and decided that "America's front yard" are the words that describe it best.

The Great Mall Memorials

If the Mall is the spiritual heart of Washington, memorials are the spiritual heart of the Mall. They honor great people or events of the past and remind millions of visitors every year of the qualities that have made our country strong. The great Mall memorials are the Washington Monument, the Lincoln Memorial, the Vietnam Veterans Memorial, the Korean War Veterans Memorial, and the Ulysses S. Grant Memorial.

The Washington Monument, built to honor George Washington, the nation's first president, was the first major memorial on the Mall. To this day, and probably forever, the sky-piercing marble obelisk remains the most dramatic, the most exciting American memorial. Together with the Statue of Liberty, it is known throughout the world as a symbol

A memorable view of the Washington Monument as seen from the Vietnam Veterans Memorial

A view of the White House seen from the top of the Washington Monument

of America. At 555 feet 5 ⅛ inches (169.3 meters), the Washington Monument is the tallest masonry structure in the world. It is made of blocks of Maryland and Massachusetts marble mortared together without metal reinforcement. The marble blocks are underlain with granite. The monument weighs 90,854 tons (82,405 metric tons). Its walls vary from a thickness of 15 feet (4.6 meters) at the base to 18 inches (46 centimeters) at the top.

An elevator ride to the top of the Washington Monument is a must for many Washington visitors. From there you can enjoy a breathtaking view of the city, the Mall, and Arlington National Cemetery (across the Potomac River).

If you go at night, you can see Washington all lit up—quite an exciting spectacle. And if, before you get into the elevator, you stand close to the monument and look straight up at the great white shaft, you will know what the poet Carl Sandburg meant when he wrote, "and stone shoots into stars here." The lighted monument does seem to shoot right into the night sky and almost touch the stars. **5**

Building the Washington Monument was a long, slow process. As early as 1783 the Continental Congress proposed that a memorial to George Washington be built. And although Congress authorized the memorial, no action had been taken to build it by the time of Washington's death in 1799.

In 1833 former president James Madison and John Marshall, then chief justice of the Supreme Court, formed the Washington National Monument Society. In 1791 L'Enfant had proposed an equestrian statue of Washington, but the society did not think that was grand enough. It decided to hold a monument design competition. Architect Robert Mills, the designer of several government buildings, won the competition. His winning plan called for a 600-foot (183-meter) nearly flat-topped obelisk surrounded by a circular colonnade. Atop this circle of columns would stand a statue of George Washington riding a chariot like a Roman emperor.

Another fifteen years would pass before enough money was raised to start the monument. Then various funding and other problems halted construction. Finally, in 1880, construction began again, but not before Lieutenant Colonel Thomas L. Casey, who succeeded Mills as architect, redesigned the monument. Casey eliminated the colonnade and statue of Washington, leaving only the dramatic Egyptian-like obelisk and adding a pyramid-shaped top. The monument was completed and dedicated in 1885— thirty-seven years after its construction had begun.

Builders work on the Washington Monument.

The **Lincoln Memorial** is America's tribute to the "Great Emancipator," President Abraham Lincoln. If the Washington Monument is the most dramatic memorial on the Mall, the Lincoln Memorial is surely the most beautiful. Designed to look like a Greek temple by American architect Henry Bacon, the exterior of the memorial is built of white Colorado marble. Thirty-six columns enclose the central block of the memorial and represent the thirty-six states in the Union at the time of President Lincoln's death.

Inside the great memorial chamber sits a statue of Abraham Lincoln created by American sculptor Daniel Chester French. Despite the statue's monumental size—19 feet (5.8 meters) upon an 11-foot (3.3-meter) pedestal—the Great Emancipator seems relaxed and friendly, almost as if waiting for people to visit him. Carved from white Georgia marble, French's masterpiece captures Lincoln's deep humanity and has become one of the most-loved treasures of the American people.

On the east side of the memorial is a ground-level exhibit area and mini-theater. There you can learn about the history of the memorial and about the wisdom and courage of the man who inspired it. ▪1

The names of the thirty-six states in the Union at the time of Lincoln's death are inscribed above the memorial's colonnade.

Just 600 feet (183 meters) from the Lincoln Memorial stands the Vietnam Veterans Memorial. Across the Reflecting Pool from the Vietnam Veterans Memorial is the Korean War Veterans Memorial. Without hurrying, a person visiting the west end of the Mall can see the Lincoln Memorial, the Vietnam Veterans Memorial, and the Korean War Memorial in two or three hours.

MORE ABOUT . . .
The Lincoln Memorial

The Lincoln Memorial is beautiful at any time of year—and at any time of day or night. It is never closed. On spring and summer evenings crowds of visitors are drawn to the memorial by lights that make haunting silhouettes of the soaring marble columns. Lincoln changes, too, as the sun disappears and only artificial light falls on him. Does he seem more lonely? Is there a greater sense that he is watching over those who are there? Perhaps that is why some people seem reluctant to leave, even as the night grows older. Perhaps that is why small groups, high-school students mostly, sit on the memorial steps, talking quietly, watching fireflies glowing in the surrounding shadows.

When finally the time comes to leave, most visitors turn for a last look at Lincoln, and they read again these words that are inscribed above his head:

IN THIS TEMPLE AS IN THE HEARTS OF
THE PEOPLE FOR WHOM HE SAVED THE
UNION THE MEMORY OF ABRAHAM
LINCOLN IS ENSHRINED FOREVER

The **Vietnam Veterans Memorial** honors the men and women of the armed forces of the United States who served in the Vietnam War. The main feature of the memorial is a black granite wall. On the wall are carved the names of more than 58,000 servicemen and servicewomen who, between 1959 and 1975, died in the war or are still missing.

The Vietnam Veterans Memorial shows different faces to visitors at different times of day and evokes different moods at different times of the year. At dawn, when the first sunlight turns the white marble of the Lincoln Memorial a soft pink, the black granite of the Vietnam Veterans Memorial becomes warm with light. At night the ground lights shining on the names pro-

Hundreds of roses line the Vietnam Veterans Memorial on Father's Day.

The Vietnam Veterans Memorial is one of the most popular memorials on the Mall.

duce a comforting glow. When snow blankets the ground, the black granite gleams and casts an almost hypnotic spell. In spring, when the grass turns green and the encircling trees are in leaf, the memorial, which itself seems a part of the earth, is most peaceful.

Thousands of people have made tracings of the names of people on the wall that have a special meaning for them. Anyone can do this. A park ranger will give you a special piece of paper made for tracing a name and will help you if the name is too high for you to reach. **2**

MORE ABOUT . . .
The Vietnam Veterans Memorial

The Vietnam War sharply divided the American people. Millions thought the United States had no business being there. Other millions felt the spread of communism in Asia had to be stopped. American servicemen and servicewomen returning from Vietnam were caught in the middle of the bitter dispute. Many veterans met with outright hostility.

Jan Scruggs, a young veteran who had been wounded in Vietnam, saw what was happening to his fellow veterans. He came to believe that America should have a memorial to honor its Vietnam veterans and that such a memorial would help to heal the nation's wounds. Beginning in 1979, Scruggs and a small group who shared his belief obtained congressional approval and raised the money for a Vietnam Veterans Memorial to be built on the Mall. A national competition for the memorial's design was won by Maya Lin, a young Chinese-American architectural student at Yale University. When her simple design for a granite wall etched with names was first printed in newspapers and magazines, some people were upset, calling it "unheroic" and even "a black gash of shame." But since its dedication in November 1982, the Vietnam Veterans Memorial has been acclaimed as one of the world's great war memorials. It is one of the most visited memorials in Washington, D.C., and, as Jan Scruggs believed, it has helped heal the nation.

The Korean War Veterans Memorial was completed and dedicated in 1995. It honors the almost two million American men and women who fought in the Korean War between 1950 and 1953.

Like the Vietnam Veterans Memorial, the Korean War Veterans Memorial has a black granite wall. But otherwise it is a completely different kind of memorial. The Vietnam Veterans Memorial wall of names emphasizes the tragedy of war. The Korean War Veterans Memorial wall is a mural containing more than 2,400 actual photographs—etched into the granite—representing servicemen and servicewomen who served in the Korean War area: pilots, paratroopers, tank crews, nurses, sur-geons, stretcher bearers, chaplains, and many, many more. The faces in the mural are of every racial and ethnic group in the United States: white, African American, Hispanic, Asian, Native American.

The most gripping part of the Korean War Veterans Memorial is a group of nineteen large unpolished stainless steel figures, an American combat patrol with their weapons at the ready. They are moving up a hill toward an American flag. Behind the flag, on the black granite wall, is an inscription: FREEDOM IS NOT FREE. The inscription punctuates the message of the memorial: Sometimes all Americans must come together to fight for freedom. Freedom is not free. **3**

Members of a Young Marines unit are fascinated by statues of a combat patrol that is part of the Korean War Veterans Memorial.

Mural artist Louis Nelson called the wall of photographs "the Nation's mantelpiece."

The Korean War began in 1950, only five years after World War II ended. Almost 150,000 Americans were killed, wounded, or missing in the war trying to prevent a takeover of non-Communist South Korea by Communist North Korea and Communist China. But because this war was fought so soon after that great war, which enveloped almost the entire world, the Korean War got little attention. As a result, it has often been called the Forgotten War.

President Bill Clinton aimed to change that idea when he spoke to a large group of veterans at the Korean War Veterans Memorial on June 25, 2000, the fiftieth anniversary of the beginning of the Korean War. In his speech Mr. Clinton said that "looking back through the long lens of history, it is clear that the stand America took in Korea was indispensable to our ultimate victory in the Cold War. Because we stood our ground in Korea, the Soviet Union drew a clear lesson that America would fight for freedom."

The president concluded his message by saying to all veterans of the Korean War: "You proved to all humanity just how good our nation can be at its best. You showed us, through your example, that freedom is not free, but can be maintained. Today, our fellow Americans say: We remember, and we are very grateful." And now the Korean War Veterans Memorial, in its place of honor on the Mall, will help our nation remember.

The Ulysses S. Grant Memorial pays tribute to the man who commanded the Union forces during the last year of the Civil War and later became the eighteenth president of the United States. The memorial is located at the eastern end of the Mall, on First Street, just below the U. S. Capitol. In front of the memorial is a wide reflecting pool.

The memorial stands on a marble platform 252 feet (77 meters) long and 71 feet (22 meters) wide. Centered on the platform, atop a 22-foot (7-meter) marble pedestal, is a bronze statue of General Grant sitting astride his war horse *Cincinnatus*. (Cincinnatus was a Roman general of the fifth century B.C.) The statue is 17 feet (5 meters) high and weighs 10,700 pounds (4,858 kilograms). General Grant is wearing his battle uniform, slouch hat, but no sword. A single word—GRANT—is etched in the marble pedestal.

On both sides of Grant's statue are sculptures dramatizing the bitter battles fought to save the Union. One portrays a fierce cavalry charge, while the other shows a running battery of artillery. **14**

Millions of foreign visitors to the Mall every year get a very special look at America. Here a Japanese tour group poses beneath the Ulysses S. Grant Memorial with the U. S. Capitol as a backdrop.

The Grant memorial was proposed in 1895 by the Society of the Army of Tennessee, Grant's old command. American sculptor Henry Merwin Shrady, who devoted the last twenty years of his life to the work, submitted the winning design for the memorial. To this day, Grant's statue is considered one of the finest bronze sculptures by an American artist. It is the second largest equestrian statue in the world. The largest is the statue of Italy's King Victor Emanuel II in Rome.

The Grant memorial was dedicated on April 27, 1922, the one hundredth anniversary of Grant's birth. The keynote address at the dedication ceremony was given by General of the Armies John Pershing, who led American forces in World War I. In a curious footnote of history, the Lincoln Memorial, at the other end of the Mall, was dedicated a month later on Memorial Day, May 30, 1922.

The bronze sculpture of General Grant at the Ulysses S. Grant Memorial on the Mall is the second largest equestrian statue in the world.

A fierce cavalry charge is part of the Grant Memorial.

25

3 Thank You, Mr. Smithson

The Smithsonian Institution is the largest museum complex in the world. It consists of sixteen museums and art galleries plus a zoo. Nine of the Smithsonian's museums and art galleries are on the Mall.

Pierre Charles L'Enfant never envisioned great museums, art galleries, and national memorials on the Mall. But it is easy to believe that if he could see the Smithsonian buildings today, he would approve. L'Enfant loved the United States, his adopted country; and in the Mall museums and galleries of the Smithsonian, art and other American treasures have been gathered and are being held in trust for the American people. Mark Twain called the Smithsonian "America's Attic." Like an attic, it is stuffed full of treasures. But, unlike most attics, the Smithsonian museums arrange and display everything beautifully.

The Smithsonian Building, 1000 Jefferson Drive, SW, was designed by famous architect James Renwick Jr. in the colorful style of twelfth century European architecture. Built of red sandstone from Seneca, Maryland, and completed in 1855, the building for many years housed all Smithsonian Institution activities: museum exhibitions, research, public lectures, and library. The Smithsonian Building has survived fire and attempts to change its architecture and stands on the Mall today as a colorful part of Washington's landscape. It is known to everyone as the Castle. It now serves mainly as an information center where visitors can go to find out about ongoing Smithsonian exhibitions and programs on the Mall. **7**

In addition to the Smithsonian Castle, the Smithsonian museums and galleries

Smithsonian Castle in early morning light

on the Mall are the Arthur M. Sackler Gallery, the Freer Gallery of Art, the Arts and Industries Building, The Hirshhorn Museum and Sculpture Garden, the National Air and Space Museum, the National Museum of African Art, the National Museum of American History, and the National Museum of Natural History. Also part of the Smithsonian is the S. Dillon Ripley Center, which houses many of the Smithsonian offices and holds an International Gallery.

The buildings that house the Smithsonian collections line both sides of the Mall, and each museum and gallery offers the visitor a rich feast.

The Arts and Industries Building, 900 Jefferson Drive, SW, has a special place among Smithsonian buildings. Opened in 1881, it is the second oldest Smithsonian building on the Mall. It was originally called the National Museum and was the first Smithsonian building designed exclusively to hold exhibits and

How did there come to be a Smithsonian Institution?

The story begins with a wealthy Englishman named James Smithson who died in 1829. A distinguished scientist, Smithson had spent his life studying chemistry and mineralogy. In his will, Smithson left his entire fortune of over $500,000 to the United States government. Smithson's will was very clear about how the money was to be used. It was "to found at Washington, under the name of the Smithsonian Institution, an Establishment for the increase and diffusion of knowledge."

Why did a British citizen who had never been to the United States leave his vast fortune to a faraway country not yet fifty years old? No one really knows. He may have felt that England had not given him the recognition he deserved as a scientist. He may have felt that the United States would be more likely to use his money the way he wanted it used.

The U. S. Congress accepted Smithson's bequest, and after a number of court delays, the money was transported to the United States aboard the ship *Mediator*. It came in 105 bags filled with British sovereigns, gold coins.

After the money arrived, Congress debated for several years about the best way to spend it. Some congressmen wanted to build a huge national library with the money. Senator Stephen A. Douglas of Illinois, most famous in history for debates with Abraham Lincoln about slavery and states' rights, wanted to use the money for agricultural research. Other congressmen wanted to support existing universities with it. Fortunately, John Quincy Adams, who had returned to Congress as a representative from Massachusetts after serving as president, argued throughout the years of debate to honor James Smithson's wish.

Finally, on August 10, 1846, President James Polk signed a bill creating a Smithsonian Institution dedicated to research and public information. Less than a year later, on May 1, 1847, amid much ceremony, the cornerstone for the Smithsonian Institution Building on the Mall was laid.

museum collections. Over the years the collections were distributed to newly built Smithsonian museums. It is a landmark structure of red brick and Ohio sandstone designed in a high Victorian style.

Today, the Arts and Industries Building features changing science, art, history, and technology exhibits from museums and art galleries around the world. Popular with children is the Discovery Theater which presents fun programs—films, plays, music. And right outside is the Smithsonian carousel! **10**

The Arts and Industries Building is the second oldest Smithsonian building on the Mall. When it opened in 1881, it was called the National Museum and was the first Smithsonian building designed exclusively to hold exhibits and museum collections.

A carousel at the Smithsonian? Yes, it has been going around and around near the Smithsonian Castle for years.

The Hirshhorn Museum, Independence Avenue and Seventh Street, SW, is devoted entirely to modern art and houses a huge collection of artworks given to the Smithsonian by American financier Joseph H. Hirshhorn. Many

A view of the circular Hirshhorn Museum. The sculpture group on the lawn by Juan Muñoz is called <u>Conversation Piece</u>.

other works of modern art have been added since the museum opened in 1974. The museum collection now totals more than ten thousand pieces.

Paintings by Mary Cassatt, Edward Hopper, Jackson Pollock, and Andy Warhol are among the many great works that can be seen here. Sculptures by almost all of the modern masters are also featured. With its wide walking areas, large windows with Mall views, and comfortable chairs for viewers who need a moment's rest, the Hirshhorn is probably the "friendliest" museum in Washington. And its circular shape makes it one of the most eye-catching buildings on the Mall. **12**

The Arthur M. Sackler Gallery, 1050 Independence Avenue, SW, and the **Freer Gallery of Art**, Jefferson Drive at Twelfth Street, SW, are both museums devoted to Asian art. These museums are fascinating to anyone interested in the art of China, Japan, Korea, the Middle East, and

The entrance to the Arthur M. Sackler Gallery

Interior of the Arthur M. Sackler Gallery lobby showing cut-out archway window with various Asian art from India

India. The exhibits include Chinese paintings, jades, and bronzes; Japanese and Korean ceramics and lacquerware, both ancient and modern; Indian sculpture; and Islamic metalware.

Both galleries have programs for young people. You can find out what's current by calling or stopping by the Smithsonian Castle. On one visit, you might get to make string puppets or learn a century-old way to hand-color photographs. On another, you might get to go on a scavenger hunt in the galleries to find flying creatures in the exhibits—angels, dragons, Egyptian gods. 8 9

The National Museum of African Art, 950 Independence Avenue, SW, has many outstanding examples of masks, headdresses, statues, and other art from Malawi, Ghana, Ivory Coast, Liberia, Nigeria, Congo, Angola, and other sub-Saharan African countries. The museum also has regular programs featuring African music, folktales, dress, and other elements of African culture. Anyone with an interest in the relationship between African and American cultures should not miss a visit to this museum.

The great modern artist Pablo Picasso once declared that African sculpture "has

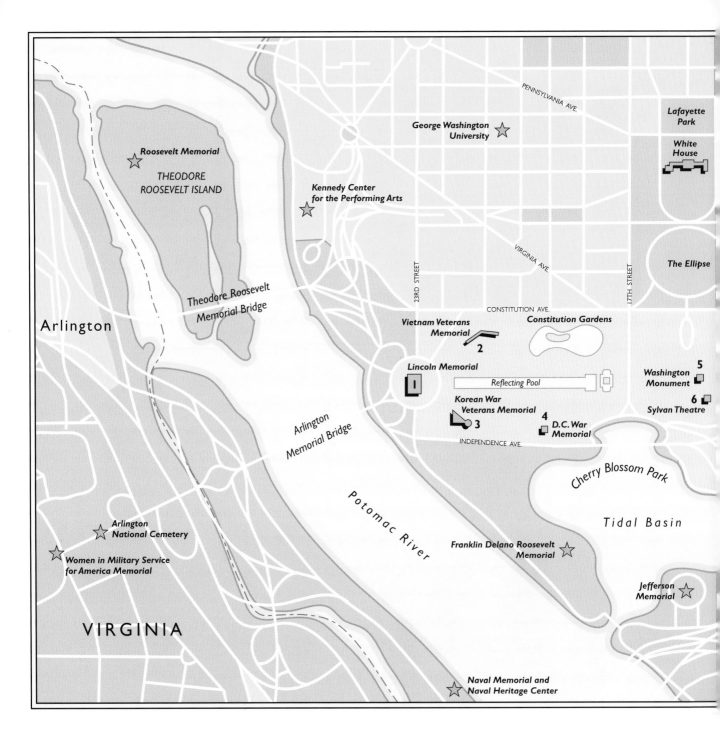

Lafayette Park

White House

George Washington University

PENNSYLVANIA AVE.

The Ellipse

VIRGINIA AVE.

Kennedy Center for the Performing Arts

Roosevelt Memorial

THEODORE ROOSEVELT ISLAND

23RD STREET

17TH STREET

CONSTITUTION AVE.

Constitution Gardens

Vietnam Veterans Memorial   2

Washington Monument   5

Theodore Roosevelt Memorial Bridge

Lincoln Memorial   1

Reflecting Pool

Sylvan Theatre   6

Arlington

Korean War Veterans Memorial   3

4   D.C. War Memorial

INDEPENDENCE AVE.

Arlington Memorial Bridge

Cherry Blossom Park

Tidal Basin

Potomac River

Arlington National Cemetery

Women in Military Service for America Memorial

Franklin Delano Roosevelt Memorial

Jefferson Memorial

VIRGINIA

Naval Memorial and Naval Heritage Center

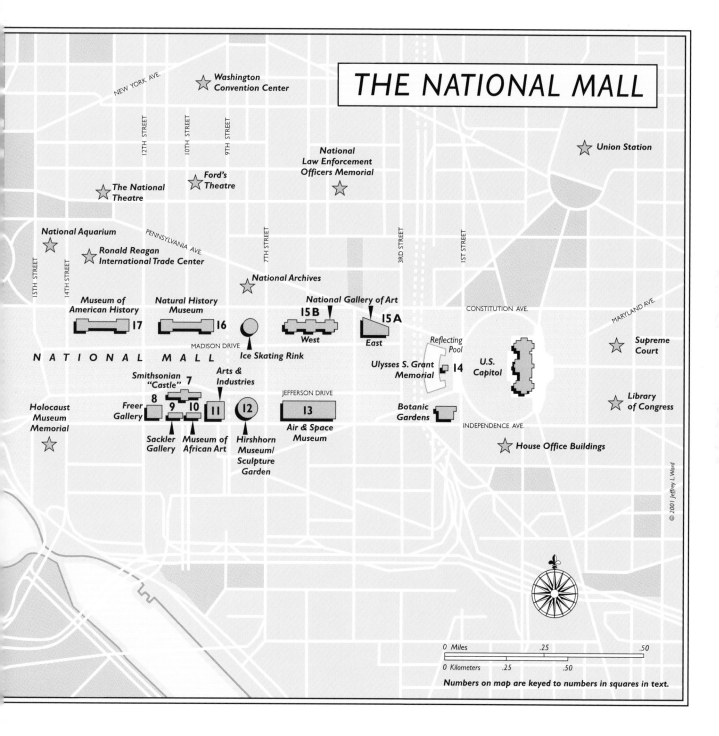

THE NATIONAL MALL

NEW YORK AVE.

⭐ Washington
Convention Center

12TH STREET

10TH STREET

9TH STREET

⭐ Union Station

National
Law Enforcement
Officers Memorial

⭐ Ford's
Theatre

⭐ The National
Theatre

PENNSYLVANIA AVE.

7TH STREET

3RD STREET

1ST STREET

⭐ National Aquarium

⭐ Ronald Reagan
International Trade Center

MARYLAND AVE.

15TH STREET

14TH STREET

⭐ National Archives

National Gallery of Art

CONSTITUTION AVE.

⭐ Supreme
Court

Museum of
American History

17

Natural History
Museum

16

15 B

West

15 A

East

Reflecting
Pool

U.S.
Capitol

MADISON DRIVE

Ice Skating Rink

Ulysses S. Grant
Memorial

14

⭐ Library
of Congress

N A T I O N A L   M A L L

Smithsonian
"Castle" **7**

Arts &
Industries

JEFFERSON DRIVE

Holocaust
Museum
Memorial

Freer
Gallery

8

9 **10** **11**

12

13

Air & Space
Museum

Botanic
Gardens

INDEPENDENCE AVE.

Sackler
Gallery

Museum of
African Art

Hirshhorn
Museum/
Sculpture
Garden

⭐ House Office Buildings

⭐

© 2001 Jeffrey L Ward

0 Miles		.25		.50

0 Kilometers		.25		.50

Numbers on map are keyed to numbers in squares in text.

A seventeenth-century Benin Bronze masterpiece (Nigeria) dominates this exhibit room in the Museum of African Art.

Sculpture of the Congo and other Central African areas are displayed in the Museum of African Art.

never been surpassed." At their best, traditional African woodcarvings, primarily from West Africa and Central Africa, are among the world's most powerful art. **10**

The underground **S. Dillon Ripley Center**, named for a former secretary of the Smithsonian, holds **The International Gallery**. This gallery features changing exhibits from different parts of the world. For example, one exhibit commemorated the three hundredth anniversary of the invention of the piano with displays of original early pianos from Europe.

The National Museum of American History, Fourteenth Street and Constitution Avenue, NW, offers three floors of exhibitions that tell the story of our nation's rich social, cultural, industrial, and scientific heritage. Exhibits provide insights into what our nation was like in colonial times and carry you through the centuries and right up to the present with exhibitions about the information age. You can learn about the African-American experience in the 1800s, immigration, and how communities have changed over time.

You can see a wide range of fascinating objects of Americana, including keepsakes

The aboveground entrance to the S. Dillon Ripley Center

Both the Sackler Gallery and the Museum of African Art are underground. You can wander through room after room of beautiful exhibits knowing that the lovely Enid A. Haupt Garden is right over your head! Also in this underground area is the S. Dillon Ripley Center.

left at the Vietnam Veterans Memorial, the flag that inspired "The Star-Spangled Banner," Thomas Edison's original lightbulb, Dorothy's Ruby Slippers from *The Wizard of Oz*, a selection of gowns worn by First Ladies, and Muhammad Ali's boxing gloves.

In addition, the museum offers demonstration centers and two hands-on centers.

In the Hands On History Room you can climb on and pedal a high-wheel bicycle, send a message by telegraph, and relive history in many other ways. In the Hands On Science Center you can investigate how the Star-Spangled Banner has been preserved, measure radioactive hot spots, use lasers to measure distance, and much, much more.

Parade day in front of
The National Museum
of American History

One of the museum's most popular features is a giant 1401 locomotive. It was brought by rail to within ten blocks of the museum, transferred to a tractor-trailer, hauled to the building, moved inside on temporary tracks, rotated on a huge turntable, and finally lowered in place. **17**

Millions of visitors flock to the **National Museum of Natural History**, Tenth Street and Constitution Avenue, NW, every year for a simple reason: It is one of the world's great centers for learning about human beings and the natural world we live in. Here you can learn about the origins of humankind and the development of world cultures. You can see displays of ancient and modern mammals, birds, reptiles, insects, and sea creatures. In the Discovery Room you can touch and hold live insects and spiders—including tarantulas. You can see (but not touch!) the Hope Diamond, the world's largest blue diamond, in the Janet Annenberg Hooker Hall of Geology, Gems, and Minerals.

Want to visit a triceratops? Just go to the Dinosaur Hall. There you can see not only triceratops but other dinosaurs as well. And when you enter the museum

The National Museum of American History is a huge building, approximately 750,000 square feet (69,675 square meters). Besides the three main exhibition levels, the museum contains a basement, two levels of offices, and a mechanical penthouse. When it first opened in 1964, it was called The Museum of History and Technology. Its name was changed in 1980.

The National Museum of Natural History

you will come face-to-face with a record 8-ton (7.3 metric tons) bush elephant.

You will recognize the Museum of Natural History by its magnificent dome that you can see from many places on the Mall. **16**

Since the **National Air and Space Museum**, Independence Avenue and Seventh Street, SW, was opened to the public on July 4, 1976, it has been at the very top of places to visit in Washington, D.C. The huge building is a virtual hangar of pink Tennessee marble and steel holding the whole history of man's dream to fly.

The twenty-three galleries of this huge museum are arranged to give you the feeling that you are seeing, even taking part in, the development of air and space flight. Galleries are devoted to Milestones

A view of the west side of the National Air and Space Museum. The sculpture is Sol De Witt's <u>Four-Sided Pyramid.</u>

One of the Air and Space Museum's many galleries devoted to Milestones of Flight

of Flight and the Space Race (with the Soviet Union). Tubular steel roof beams support the enormous weight of the exhibits. Among the hundreds of flight and space treasures you can see are the original plane built by Wilbur and Orville Wright, the single-engine *Spirit of St. Louis* in which Charles Lindbergh made the first transatlantic flight, the Apollo 11 Command Module, and the Hubble Space Telescope test vehicle.

In the Air and Space Museum you can watch flight and space travel films on a mammoth screen—five stories high. You can also attend planetarium shows that explore the workings of our universe. Do you like or build model airplanes? Here you can see hundreds of models of every type.

The Smithsonian is many things. It is a place of learning, but it is also a place to have fun. It is a place to look into the past and see into the future. **13**

The National Gallery of Art

The National Gallery of Art is located in two huge buildings between Third and Seventh streets on the Constitution Avenue side of the Mall. It is not a part of the Smithsonian Institution, but like the Smithsonian, the National Gallery of Art had its beginning with the generous gift of one man. That man was Andrew W. Mellon, American financier and art collector, who began collecting art during the 1920s with the idea of forming an art gallery for the nation in Washington, D.C. In 1937

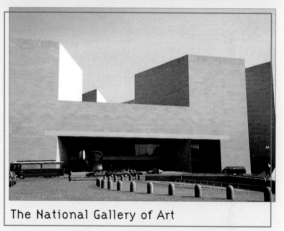

The National Gallery of Art

Congress created the National Gallery of Art by accepting the Mellon gift of hundreds of valuable paintings and other art as well as the money to construct the building to house the collection.

In 1969 Paul Mellon, son of Andrew Mellon, and Ailsa Mellon Bruce donated funds to build a new East Building for the National Gallery of Art. The East Building, designed by famous architect I. M. Pei, is one of the most spectacular buildings on the Mall. It was completed, dedicated, and opened to the public in 1978.

The National Gallery of Art concentrates on collecting the work of European and American artists from the late Middle Ages to the present. **15**

4 Gardens, Grass, and Many Paths

The National Mall that Pierre Charles L'Enfant dreamed of in the late eighteenth century was a long, wide grassy area made for walking. Although today's Mall contains great memorials and museums, it remains remarkably true to L'Enfant's original vision.

Today's Mall is a place of beautiful lawns and miles of tree-lined paths that lead to lovely gardens. The sweeping lawn that stretches between the Capitol and the Washington Monument is 300 feet (91.5 meters) wide. Paths cross it at regular intervals, but no permanent building or other structure stands on it. It is truly a "grand promenade vista."

Washington residents and visitors use the Mall's lawns and grassy stretches for picnicking, sunbathing, playing Frisbee, flying kites, romping with their dogs.

Summer or winter, the Mall is a place to play.

Walkers and joggers fill the Mall's many paths year round—in any kind of weather. The Mall truly belongs to the people.

Constitution Gardens is a quiet park within the Mall bordering Constitution Avenue between the Washington Monument and the Lincoln Memorial. Cars stream by on the busy thoroughfare, but long rows of trees shield the park from noise. This section of the Mall is a wide area of grass with gentle knolls and many paths, one of which leads to the Vietnam

The large pond in Constitution Gardens attracts ducks and people.

Veterans Memorial. Near the center of Constitution Gardens is a large pond where ducks swim. The bolder ones cruise near the edge, hoping for handouts from picnickers. A small island in the pond is connected to the land by a bridge. On the island is a memorial dedicated to the fifty-six signers of the Declaration of Independence. Each signer's name, signature, and occupation is carved into a block of stone.

Constitution Gardens draws many bird-watchers. It is what they call a "migrant trap," a wide green space in the midst of a large city that attracts birds, particularly in the spring and fall.

The wood thrush, a brown bird with a white throat and chest, is the official bird of the District of Columbia. It returns to Washington in late April from its wintering grounds in the forests of Mexico. Its flutelike song is one of the lovely sounds of spring on the Mall.

On the south side of the Reflecting Pool is an area called **Ash Woods**. It contains some of the largest non-elm trees on the Mall. It also has many colorful azaleas and other flowering shrubs and bushes that attract migrant birds.

The Korean War Veterans Memorial is located in Ash Woods. Farther to the east, nestled among the trees and noticed only by strollers on the nearby path, is a small memorial with Doric (Greek)-type columns that honors veterans from the District of Columbia who served in World War I. The memorial was dedicated on Armistice Day (now Veterans Day), November 11, 1931. 4

The most beautiful gardens on the Mall are the ones near the Smithsonian complex of buildings. Of these, the **Enid A. Haupt Garden** is probably best known.

The almost forgotten District of Columbia War Veterans Memorial on the south side of the Mall's Reflecting Pool is beautiful with spring flowers surrounding it.

The Haupt Garden fills the center of a quadrangle formed by the Castle, the Arts and Industries Building, the Freer Gallery, and the entrances to the Museum of African Art and the Sackler Gallery. The Haupt Garden, in fact, grows on the roof of the Sackler and the African Art Museum's

In late April, Hummingbird Tulips join ever-present pansies in the Enid A. Haupt Garden.

underground display galleries! Elaborate cast-iron gates, designed in 1849 by James Renwick, and red sandstone pillars decorate the Independence Avenue entrance to the quadrangle and the garden.

The Haupt Garden covers 4.2 acres (1.7 hectares). Its flower beds form a pattern with elaborate shapes and designs (parterre). During each season of the year these beds brim with thousands of flowers: pansies in the spring, for example; ornamental cabbage in the fall; celosia and marigolds in the summer. Throughout the garden are beautiful antique garden furnishings.

The Haupt Garden also has an Oriental garden area near the Sackler Gallery and a North African garden area near the African Art Museum. Two other smaller gardens in the quadrangle area feature roses, irises, and other bulb flowers.

The **Mary Livingston Ripley Garden** was the inspiration of Mrs. S. Dillon Ripley, wife of the Smithsonian's eighth sec-

The Mary Livingston Ripley Garden

retary. A lifelong plant scholar, Mrs. Ripley conceived the idea of a "fragrant garden" to be located along the eastern side of the Arts and Industries Building. The Garden contains more than eight hundred varieties of plants, among them candytuft, alyssum "Basket of Gold," windflowers, saffron crocuses, and woodland phlox.

Not all gardens on the Mall feature flowers. When the Hirshhorn Museum opened in 1974, the Mall was enriched by a *new* kind of garden—a sunken outdoor sculpture garden. **The Hirshhorn Sculpture Garden** displays more than sixty works in bronze and steel by the greatest sculptors of Europe and America: Alberto Giacometti, Joan Miró, Henry Moore, and David Smith, among many others. The sculptures are set among trees, grass, and vines that cover the garden walls.

Another sculpture garden, the **National Gallery of Art Sculpture Garden**, was dedicated on May 19, 1999, and accepted for the nation by then First Lady Hillary Rodham Clinton.

Located on the Constitution Avenue side of the Mall between Seventh and Ninth streets, the Sculpture Garden is a

At the Hirshhorn Sculpture Garden, this young man may be wondering if the rider in Marino Marini's bronze statue <u>Horse and Rider</u> will end up with his arm in a sling!

place of greenery and imagination. It has abundant space—6.1 acres (2.5 hectares)— and a large central fountain ringed by linden trees. Perennials, ground covers, shrubs, and flowering trees provide a friendly setting for the seventeen pieces of modern sculpture carefully placed throughout the garden.

The sculptures on view have been selected from the work of master artists, mostly American, produced since World

44

War II. Some of the sculptures have abstract or unusual shapes, and you wonder what the artist is trying to communicate. But they are all interesting to look at.

Some of the artists seem to be having fun. One visitor favorite is Barry Flanagan's *Thinker on a Rock*, a giant bronze rabbit, leaning forward, resting a paw against his chin. The sculpture is a parody—a spoof—of one of the world's most famous statues, Auguste Rodin's *The Thinker*.

Other favorites in the Sculpture Garden are a huge spider made of bronze by Louise Bourgeois, and *House I* by Roy Lichtenstein. Lichtenstein's brightly painted house is an optical illusion—although flat, it appears to be three-dimensional.

Thinker on a Rock sculpture

Some visitors to the National Gallery of Art Sculpture Garden are a bit startled to suddenly come upon the huge bronze Spider by American sculptor Louise Bourgeois.

The U.S. Botanic Garden, located at the eastern end of the Mall along First Street, is the oldest garden of its kind in North America. George Washington suggested such a garden as early as 1796. In 1820, Congress authorized a botanic garden for the display, scientific study, and growth of plants from other countries that might be of benefit to the American people. The U. S. Botanic Garden was main-

The U.S. Botanic Garden features a wide variety of tropical, subtropical, and desert plants.

tained in various places in Washington, D.C., until 1933 when it was moved to its present location on the Mall. At that time a conservatory (greenhouse) for the plants was built, with two outside acres for additional plants.

The U. S. Botanic Garden features thousands of species of tropical, subtropical, and desert plants. Its collection of orchids—over five thousand different types—is particularly outstanding. Annual flower shows feature such exotic plants as birds-of-paradise, hibiscus, and century plants, as well as more familiar flowers such as tulips, chrysanthemums, roses, and poppies. Flower shows at the Botanic Garden in 1996 attracted almost three quarters of a million viewers.

Roy Lichtenstein's <u>House I</u> in the National Gallery of Art Sculpture Garden looks real enough, but is it? Visitors are in for a surprise.

Some of the sculptures puzzle visitors, particularly, *Typewriter Eraser, Scale X*, by Claes Oldenburg and Coosje van Bruggen. It is a very large sculpture, made of painted stainless steel and fiberglass, of a kind of eraser used to correct mistakes made on a typewriter. Although the eraser was common throughout the world for much of the nineteenth and twentieth centuries, few young people of the computer age have ever seen the strange-looking object. The idea for the sculpture came to Oldenburg from his days as a

Typewriter Eraser, Scale X by Claes Oldenburg and Coosje van Bruggen

young boy playing with the typewriter erasers in his father's office.

Every garden on the Mall may not be what you are looking for, but some of them are sure to be.

5 Special Times on the Mall

What better place to be on America's birthday than in America's front yard? Every year on the Fourth of July as many as half a million people decide there is no better place and make their way to the Mall in Washington, D.C. Many people plan their Washington vacation to include Independence Day, knowing what a special day it is in the nation's capital. Thousands of others drive for several hours, from as far away as Ohio, New Jersey, and North Carolina to be a part of the fun and excitement.

The big attraction is the fireworks display that bursts for twenty minutes over and around the Washington Monument at about nine o'clock every Fourth of July night. At that time the sky flames as almost four thousand shells are propelled upward and explode every two

seconds during the main part of the show. As the shells explode, thousands of "shooting stars" fill the sky. As one sixth-grade girl described the moment, "The best ones poof out and look like a big Koosh ball." The whole time a machine-gun-like noise fills the night as the shells are fired and break apart. When the show is over, the huge crowd around the Washington Monument applauds and shouts its appreciation.

Crowds of people pour onto the grounds of the Washington Monument to watch the fireworks spectacular, but there are many other good watching places. You can get good views from the steps of the Lincoln Memorial, the west steps of the Capitol, and the open Mall areas on both sides of the Washington Monument. Some people park on Constitution Avenue and watch from the top of their car. Others watch from boats on the Potomac River.

The Fourth of July on the Mall is far more than fireworks. Families begin arriving by midmorning bringing blankets, beach umbrellas, lawn chairs, and baskets full of sandwiches, baked beans, potato salad, and deviled eggs—all the good things of a Fourth of July picnic. Even with the big crowd, you can still find space on the Mall to play soccer, throw a baseball, or just run around.

And the Mall offers still more on Independence Day. Every year a Fourth of July parade begins at midday and marches most of the length of Constitution Avenue. Bands from different parts of the country always take part. Military bands hold concerts on the steps of the Air and Space Museum and at the Sylvan Theatre near the Washington Monument. The National Symphony Orchestra plays on the west lawn of the Capitol. Many visitors go to the National Archives on Constitution Avenue between Seventh and Ninth streets, NW, to see the Declaration of Independence,

Spectacular fireworks burst over the Washington Monument on the Fourth of July, 1999. The scaffolding around the monument adds to the dramatic effect.

the Constitution, and the Bill of Rights that are on display there.

One Mall visitor on Independence Day 1999 was Sridhar Vallepalli, who came for the last Fourth of July celebration of the twentieth century. Originally from India, Vallepalli now lives and works in New Jersey. "This is such an important day in American history," he told a *Washington Post* reporter. And Vallepalli might have been speaking for everyone on the Mall that day when he said that "it was the only place to be."

The **Smithsonian Festival of American Folklife** also brings visitors flocking to the Mall each year for ten days the last week of June and the first week of July. The Smithsonian carefully plans each year's program to let visitors see, hear, and feel the richness of American folk cultures.

A group of Cape Verdean-Americans from Massachusetts performs at the Smithsonian Festival of American Folklife on the Mall.

Is this the Mall in Washington, D.C.? Indeed, it is. One year Iowans came to the Festival of American Folklife and showed in many ways what life in their state is like.

One of the most memorable gatherings ever to occur on the Mall was the civil rights "March on Washington for Jobs and Freedom" in 1963. Hundreds of thousands of Americans, of all colors, came from all over the country for the rally, which concluded with Dr. Martin Luther King Jr. delivering his now famous "I Have a Dream" speech at the Lincoln Memorial. Dr. King spoke of his dream of a day when black and white people of America "will be able to work together, to pray together, to struggle together."

The "March on Washington" crowd stretched from the Lincoln Memorial to the Washington Monument.

Since Dr. King's famous speech, the Mall has become increasingly the place where people come to express their thoughts. Between late April and early July 2000, for example, the Mall hosted large demonstrations for Earth Day (stressing environmental concerns), the Millennium March for Equality, the Million Mom March for gun control, and a right-to-life rally.

The Mall is America's front yard, and American groups with social causes want to be seen and heard there.

Native American women dancers at a major 1992 conference entitled "Native Voices on the Mall." The conference was to call attention to American Indian needs and concerns.

The Folklife Festival program varies from year to year with groups from a number of different parts of the country taking part. One year Mississippi Delta groups might present their crafts, music, dances, food, and storytelling. Another year Navajo women demonstrate their rug-weaving skills. At the 1998 festival the state of Wisconsin showed occupational folklore: dairy farm milking, cheese and sausage making, cranberry and ginseng growing. At the 2000 festival cowboys from the Rio Grande roped cattle on the Mall!

Activities start in the morning and go well into the night. The festival offers a full program on the Fourth of July, which makes going to the Mall on that special day even more exciting.

The National Mall in the Twenty-first Century

The National Mall as we know it today developed over a period of two centuries. In the nineteenth century the Smithsonian Institution began its presence on the Mall; the Washington Monument was built; and land reclaimed from the Potomac River marshes extended the Mall westward. In the twentieth century the great Mall memorials were built; the U.S. Botanical Garden was relocated on the Mall; the Smithsonian museums and the National Gallery of Art were built; and the Mall became a place of beautiful gardens, grass, and walking paths.

Is the Mall now complete? The answer, of course, is no. Just as our nation changes, so will the Mall.

Scheduled to open on the Mall in 2004 are a new Smithsonian museum, the National Museum of the American Indian, and a National World War II Memorial. The National Museum of the American Indian is to be located between the Air and Space Museum and the U.S. Botanic Garden in a new 260,000-square-foot (24,154-square-meter) building. Museum exhibits drawn from a collection of over 800,000 artifacts

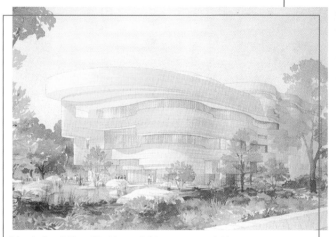

Model of the National Museum of the American Indian

and art objects will tell the story of the achievements of all natives of the Western Hemisphere.

Congress has approved a National World War II Memorial for the Mall. Many people feel that this memorial is long overdue because World War II was the most important turning point of the twentieth century. The memorial will honor the Americans who fought in the war and recognize the triumph of democracy over tyranny. The World War II Memorial will be located between the Washington Monument and the Reflecting Pool.

Congress has also approved construction of a Black Patriots Memorial on the Mall. It is to honor the five thousand black slaves and freedmen who fought and died for American independence during the Revolutionary War as well as all African Americans who have risked their lives in the cause of freedom. The memorial is to be located in Constitution Gardens on the north side of the Reflecting Pool.

Other than these, it is unlikely that any new memorials will be built on the Mall in the foreseeable future. The influential National Capital Planning Commission and related organizations that advise Congress on the design and location of memorials are deeply concerned that additional memorials would clutter the Mall and detract from the ones that are now there. The commission recommends that no new memorials be built on the Mall or on the land between the White House and the Jefferson Memo-

Model of the World War II Memorial

rial. (An exception is the Martin Luther King Jr. Memorial already approved for a site on the Tidal Basin across from the Jefferson Memorial.)

Only Congress can authorize a memorial to be built on the Mall. Pressures on Congress by groups wanting to build memorials are very great, but the lawmakers probably will follow the advice of the National Capital Planning Commission. As the commission has pointed out, other good locations still exist for new memorials in the District of Columbia.

But the absence of new memorials does not mean that the National Mall will not change, grow, and become even more beautiful in the future. The great museums and art galleries will continue to increase their collections. And the present treasures of the Mall may be made even more beautiful and appealing to visitors in the new century. For example, the Washington Monument was cleaned and repaired between 1999 and 2001 and renovation and reconstruction of the Botanic Garden conservatory began then. A 3-acre (1.2-hectare) addition to the National Garden promises to be a

Famous American architect Michael Graves created a dramatic work of art by designing a fabric sheathing—lit with interior lights—to decorate the scaffolding around the Washington Monument during its repair. Graves's design was a pleasing temporary addition to the Washington skyline and was much appreciated by visitors who otherwise would have been disappointed to see an ugly scaffold around the monument. The scaffold was taken down before the July 4, 2000, celebration, after having been up for about a year.

showcase for unusual, useful, and ornamental plants that grow well in the mid-Atlantic region.

In 2001 Jan Scruggs, president of the Vietnam Veterans Memorial Fund, called attention to the seldom-visited, almost-forgotten District of Columbia Veterans War Memorial on the Mall. With only some cleaning and renovation, Scruggs pointed out, it could be made into a beautiful small memorial and rededicated as a National World War I Memorial for all American men and women who served and died in the "war to end all wars." Scruggs wrote: "The doughboys of World War I won't be there to see the day when they are remembered, yet their sacrifices must be recognized and commemorated—just like those of the veterans of Vietnam, Korea, and World War II."

The National Mall is the responsibility of the National Park Service. As increasing millions flock to the Mall in the twenty-first century, the Park Service vows to be ready for the challenge of keeping America's front yard beautiful for the American people.

Visitor Information about the National Mall

The Lincoln Memorial, Vietnam Veterans Memorial, Korean War Veterans Memorial, and Ulysses S. Grant Memorial are open to the public twenty-four hours a day every day of the year. Park rangers are on duty at the Lincoln, Vietnam Veterans, and Korean War Veterans memorials from 8:00 A.M. to 11:45 P.M. every day except December 25. Park rangers are sometimes on duty at the Grant Memorial.

Summer hours for going to the top of the Washington Monument begin the first Sunday in April, and the monument is open from 8:00 A.M. to 11:45 P.M. Winter hours begin the day after Labor Day, and the monument is open 9:00 A.M. to 4:45 P.M. Tickets are required. Free tickets can be obtained at the kiosk on the Fifteenth Street side of the monument. During the summer, the kiosk opens at 7:30 A.M., during the winter at 8:30 A.M. One person can obtain a maximum of six tickets. Advance tickets can be obtained through the National Park Reservation Service at 1-800-967-2283 or at www.reservations.nps.gov. There is a $1.50 convenience charge per ticket and a $.50 handling fee per order.

Smithsonian Institution museums on the Mall are open daily, except December 25, from 10:00 A.M. to 5:30 P.M., unless otherwise noted. Admission to all Smithsonian museums is free, unless otherwise noted. The Smithsonian Information Center, in the Castle, is open daily from 9:00 A.M. to 5:30 P.M. For additional Smithsonian information, call (202) 357-2700 or (202) 357-1729; write to: Smithsonian Information, Smithsonian Institution, Room 153, Washington, DC 20560-0010, or send e-mail to info@info.si.edu.

The National Gallery of Art is open every Monday–Saturday from 10:00 A.M. to 5:00 P.M. and every Sunday from 11:00 A.M. to 6:00 P.M., except December 25 and January 1. Admission is free. For information about exhibits, call (202) 842-6353 or write to Information Office, National Gallery of Art, Washington, DC 20560.

Guided Mall tourmobiles, a concession of the National Park Service, operate daily from various Mall locations from 9:00 A.M. to 6:30 P.M (summer) and 9:30 A.M. to 4:00 P.M. (winter). Tickets are required and provide unlimited reboarding privileges. For information call (202) 554-7950.

Those interested in learning more about the National Mall should contact the National Park Service at:

National Capital Parks—Central
The National Mall
900 Ohio Drive, SW
Washington, D.C. 20024
Telephone: (202) 426-6841
Internet: www.nps.gov

Important Places of Visitor Interest Near the Mall

ARLINGTON NATIONAL CEMETERY, across Memorial Bridge. A hallowed place where thousands of American heroes are buried. Daily ceremonies are held at the Tomb of the Unknowns.

CHERRY TREES, West Potomac Park around the Tidal Basin. More than three thousand cherry trees, the first of which were given to the United States by Japan in 1912, bloom in late March or early April. The annual Cherry Blossom Festival brings thousands of visitors.

FRANKLIN DELANO ROOSEVELT MEMORIAL, West Potomac Park on Ohio Avenue. An unusual memorial, divided into four outdoor galleries, one for each of President Roosevelt's terms in office.

HOLOCAUST MUSEUM, 100 Raoul Wallenberg Place, SW. This museum memorializes the six million Jews and others who were annihilated by Nazi Germany during World War II. Not appropriate for young people under eleven.

LIBRARY OF CONGRESS, First Street and Independence Avenue, SE. (three buildings). This largest library in the world—90 million items on 540 miles (869 kilometers) of shelves—offers much more than books in its exhibit and music rooms.

NATIONAL AQUARIUM, Department of Commerce building, Fourteenth Street and Constitution Avenue, NW. The oldest public aquarium in the nation displays over 1,200 fish and other water creatures.

NATIONAL ARCHIVES, Constitution Avenue and 7th Street, NW. Among other national treasures, it houses the original Declaration of Independence, the Constitution, and the Bill of Rights.

NATIONAL LAW ENFORCEMENT OFFICERS MEMORIAL, located on Judiciary Square. The memorial honors all of America's federal, state, and local law enforcers.

THOMAS JEFFERSON MEMORIAL, at the Tidal Basin. The memorial to the nation's third president and author of the Declaration of Independence is a white marble dome-shaped rotunda in a setting of cherry trees.

U.S. CAPITOL, Capitol Hill at the east end of the Mall. Here the Senate and the House of Representatives do their work. You are welcome to visit the office of your senator or congressman. Tours of the Capitol are free, and there is much to see.

U.S. NAVY MEMORIAL AND NAVAL HERITAGE CENTER, Pennsylvania Avenue, NW, between Seventh and Ninth streets. The Naval Heritage Center is a treasure house of U.S. Naval History. In spring and summer band concerts, wreath-laying ceremonies, and other outdoor activities take place at the memorial.

U.S. SUPREME COURT, Maryland Avenue and First Street, NE, with visitor entrances on both streets. The highest court of the land where the nine supreme court justices precide offers a variety of educational programs and exhibits.

WHITE HOUSE, 1600 Pennsylvania Avenue, NW. The White House has been the home of every U.S. president except George Washington. It is open to visitors in the morning, Tuesday through Saturday. Self-guided tours are free but require timed tickets which can be obtained from the White House Visitor Center at Fifteenth and E streets, NW.

WOMEN IN MILITARY SERVICE FOR AMERICA MEMORIAL, entrance to Arlington National Cemetery. This fascinating new memorial tells the story of the contributions that women have made in all branches of the military service in times of war and peace.

For Further Information

Books and Articles

Ashabranner, Brent. *No Better Hope: What the Lincoln Memorial Means to America*. Brookfield, CT: Twenty-First Century Books, 2000.

————. *Remembering Korea: The Korean War Veterans Memorial*. Brookfield, CT: Twenty-First Century Books, 2001.

————. *Their Names to Live: What the Vietnam Veterans Memorial Means to America*. Brookfield, CT: Twenty-First Century Books, 1998.

Danzig, Barbara. "Who's Remembered in the Grant Memorial?" *The Washington Post*, March 18, 2001.

Forgey, Benjamin. "Growing Wild on the Mall," *The Washington Post*, December 31, 2000.

————. "Unwrapped Present: For America's Birthday, a Spruced-Up Monument Deserves Celebration." *The Washington Post*, July 4, 2000.

Forgey, Benjamin, and David Montgomery. "Art Under the Open Sky: National Gallery's Sculpture Garden Blooms at Last." *The Washington Post*, May 20, 1999.

Hoig, Stan. *A Capital for the Nation*. New York: Cobblehill Books, 1990.

Kent, Deborah. *Washington D.C.* (America the Beautiful series). Chicago: Children's Press, 1995.

Reps, John W. *Washington on View: The National Capital Since 1790*. Chapel Hill: The University of North Carolina Press, 1991.

Sandburg, Carl. *Complete Poems*. New York: Harcourt, Brace, & Company, 1950.

Schultz, Brigit. "'Only Place to Be': True-Blue Crowd Celebrates on the Mall." *The Washington Post*, July 5, 1999.

Scruggs, Jan. "Our Doughboys Deserve to Be Honored, Too." *The Washington Post,* August 13, 2000.

The Smithsonian Experience: Science—History—the Arts: The Treasures of the Nation. Washington, D.C.: The Smithsonian Institution, 1977.

Thomson, Peggy. *Auks, Rocks and the Odd Dinosaur: Inside Stories from the Smithsonian Museum of Natural History.* New York: Thomas Y. Crowell, 1983.

———. *The Nine-Ton Cat: Behind the Scenes at an Art Museum.* Boston: Houghton Mifflin Company, 1987.

Wheeler, Linda. "Monumental Proposal: Plan Would Ban New Memorials in Most of Mall." *The Washington Post,* September 19, 1999.

Internet

Smithsonian Institution
www.si.edu

National Park Service/National Mall
www.nps.gov/nama

National Capital Region
www.nps. gov/ncro

U. S. Geological Survey: Building Stones of Our Nation's Capital, A Walking Tour
pubs.usgs.gov/gip/stones/tour.html

Index

Page numbers in *italics* refer to illustrations.